D0524616

EARTH'S
WONDERS

First published in 2012 by
Miles Kelly Publishing Ltd
Harding's Barn, Bardfield End Green,
Thaxted, Essex, CM6 3PX, UK

Copyright © Miles Kelly Publishing Ltd 2012
This edition printed 2013

10 9 8 7 6 5 4 3 2

Publishing Director Belinda Gallagher
Creative Director Jo Cowan
Managing Editors Amanda Askew,
   Rosie McGuire
Managing Designer Simon Lee
Proofreaders Carly Blake, Claire Philip
Production Manager Elizabeth Collins
Image Manager Liberty Newton
Reprographics Stephan Davis, Thom Allaway
Assets Lorraine King

All rights reserved. No part of this publication
may be reproduced, stored in a retrieval
system, or transmitted by any means,
electronic, mechanical, photocopying,
recording or otherwise, without the prior
permission of the copyright holder.

ISBN 978-1-84810-690-1

Printed in China

British Library Cataloguing-in-Publication Data
A catalogue record for this book is available
from the British Library

Made with paper from a sustainable forest

www.mileskelly.net
info@mileskelly.net

www.factsforprojects.com

ACKNOWLEDGMENTS

The publishers would like to thank the following sources for the use
of their photographs:

KEY t=top, b=bottom, c=center, l=left, r=right
AL=Alamy, B=Bridgeman, CO=Corbis, F=Fotolia, FLPA=Frank Lane Picture Agency,
GI=Getty Images, IS=istockphoto.com, NPL=Nature Picture Library,
PL=Photolibrary, RF=Rex Features, SPL=Science Photo Library, S=Shutterstock,
TF=Topfoto

COVER Richard Nowitz/National Geographic Society/CO BACK COVER Richard
Peterson/S, Magnolia/S
1 AR Pictures/S; 2 Pedro Nogueira/S; 3(bg) Dropu/S, (strip, left to right)
fotosutra.com/S, mangostock/S, Specta/S, bumihills/S, POZZO DI BORGO
Thomas/S; 4–5 Sylvain Grandadam/GI; 6(bl) Image
Source/CO, (tr) siloto/S; 7(br) TED MEAD/GI, (tl) Vakhrushev Pavel/S, (tr) David
Wall/AL; 8–9 Radius Images/GI; 8(bl) ozoptimist/S, (tl) irin-k/S, (tr) NASA/CO;
9(br) AR Pictures/S, (cr) Gunnar Pippel/S, (tl) valdezrl/S, (tr) Joel Sartore/GI,
(tr) Steve Collender/S; 10–11 Marc Turcan/S, Brian Chase/S;
10(bl) KeystoneUSA-ZUMA/RF, (bl) Oxlock/S, (bl) Hintau Aliaksei/S,
(bl) sniegirova mariia/S, (tl) nito/S, (tl) PILart/S; 11(b) caimacanul/S,
(b) astudio/S, (br) GI, (tl) mangostock/S; 12–13 Keattikorn/S, exclusive
studio/S, (bc) Ariadne Van Zandbergen/GI, (tc) Grauvision/S; 12(bl) Lukiyanova
Natalia/frenta/S, (br) exclusive studio/S, (cl) DOELAN Yann/GI, (tl) photostudio
7/S, (tl) Kompaniets Taras/S; 13(c) Marilyn Volan/S, (br) zimmytws/S,
(cr) Carolina Biological/Visuals Unlimited/CO, (tl) haveseen/S, (tr) bonsai/S,
(tr) Graeme Shannon/S; 14–15 Theo Allofs/CO; 14(c) jspix/GI, (bl) Gavriel
Jecan/CO, (bl) Wutthichai/S; 15(cr) Luciano Candisani/Minden Pictures/FLPA,
(tl) Jurgen & Christine Sohns/FLPA/GI; 16–17 aopsan/S, George Steinmetz/SPL;
16(bl) Magnum/F, (bl) Cornelia Doerr/GI, (bl) magicinfoto/S, (br) Tony
Waltham/Robert Harding World Imagery/CO, (cl) alarik/S, (cl) Picsfive/S,
(tl) Kaspri/S; 17(bc) M.E. Mulder/S, (br) AFP/GI, (tr) George Steinmetz/SPL;
18–19 José Fuste Raga/GI; 18(tl) ErickN/S; 19(tl) Catherine Karnow/CO;
20–21 Peter Adams/JAI/CO, (c) Michael Krabs/GI; 20(b) Tadao
Yamamoto/amanaimages/CO, (b) S, (bl) Anan Kaewkhammul/S, (tr) R-studio/S;

21(br) Peter Johnson/CO, (tr) Charles Bowman/GI, (tr) Bomshtein/S;
22–23 Atlantide Phototravel/CO; 22(bl) Ken Welsh/GI, (l) Anne Kitzman/S,
(tr) Vitaly Korovin/S; 23(br) GI, (br) Alistair Scott/S, (tr) Yvette Cardozo/GI;
24–25 Oliver Lucanus/Minden Pictures/FLPA; 24(bl) ermess/S, (cl) Mazzzur/S,
(tr) Dropu/S; 25(bl) Joanne Weston/S, (br) Vlad61/S, (br) Merkushev Vasiliy/S,
(br) yui/S, (tr) Reinhard Dirscherl/GI, (tr) fotosutra.com/S; 26–27 AF
archive/AL, Filipchuk Oleg Vasiliovich/S, Borodaev/S; 26(br) AF archive/AL,
(cr) bumihills/S; 27(br) Hemis/AL, (br) Tischenko Irina/S, (tl) MVaresvuo/GI,
(tl) S, (tr) Eitan Simanor/GI; 28–29 ImageBroker/Imagebroker/FLPA, (tc) Marina
Horvat/ Imagebroker/FLPA; 28(bl) Picsfive/S; 29(br) Georg Knoll/GI, (br) Max
Topchii/S, (t) Nikki Bidgood/GI; 30–31 PlanetObserver/SPL; 30(t) David
Pickford/GI; 31(bl) Pozzo di Borgo Thomas/S, (br) Morandi Bruno/GI, (tl) Hugh
Lansdown/FLPA, (tr) ARouse/GI; 32–33(b) Paul Souders/CO, (t) Barcroft
Media/GI, (t) Roman Krochuk/S; 32(bl) Dr Juerg Alean/SPL; 33(br) Steven
Kazlowski/Science Faction/CO, (cr) Anthony Cooper/SPL; 34–35 Nejron Photo/S,
silvae/S, (c) Planet Observer/GI; 34(bl) Hefr/S, (bl) Hefr/S; 35(bl) Joe
Carini/GI, (bl) Patrick McFeeley/GI, (cr) Yuganov Konstantin/S, (tr) Ann
Cecil/GI; 36–37 Emmanuel Lattes/AL, xpixel/S; 36(bl) Visuals Unlimited,
Inc./Reinhard Dirscherl/GI, (bl) fotosutra.com/S, (br) Scottchan/S,
(l) maxstockphoto/S, (l) Malivan_Iuliia/S, (t) ronstik/S, (t) aboikis/S,
(tl) HGalina/S, (tl) irin-k/S, (tl) Scottchan/S; 37(bl) Reinhard Dirscherl/GI,
(br) inxti/S, (tr) Barcroft Media/GI, (tr) Steve Collender/S;
38–39 3355m/S, PhotoHappiness/S, (t) Andy Rouse/NPL; 38(bl) Specta/S,
(br) Mark Conlin/GI, (tl) Marilyn Volan/S, (tr) Finbarr O'Reilly/ Reuters/CO;
39(b) Stan Osolinski/GI, (bl) Seth Resnick/Science Faction/CO, (t) Nir Darom/S,
(tr) George Steinmetz/SPL

All other photographs are from: Corel, digitalSTOCK, digitalvision,
Dreamstime.com, Fotolia.com, iStockphoto.com, John Foxx, PhotoAlto,
PhotoDisc, PhotoEssentials, PhotoPro, Stockbyte

Every effort has been made to acknowledge the source and copyright
holder of each picture. The publishers apologise for any unintentional
errors or omissions.

EARTH'S WONDERS

Camilla de la Bedoyere

Consultant: John Farndon

Miles Kelly

CONTENTS

◄ On average, 38,500 cu ft (2,000 cu m) of water flows over the Victoria Falls every second, creating a mighty roar that can be heard up to 25 mi (40 km) away.

Mighty Monolith

Uluru rises majestically above a flat desert horizon in central Australia. Also known as Ayers Rock, this giant red monolith creates such an awesome spectacle—especially at dawn and dusk—that it is central to the religious faith of the indigenous people.

Island mountain

Uluru is the tip of a massive rock slab that is buried to a depth of 4 mi (6 km). Its complex history began 900 million years ago when sediments began collecting in a depression in Earth's crust. Now it is one of the last witnesses to some mammoth geological processes, including the weathering and erosion that have removed the surrounding rocks. These forces will, one day, also erase the mighty Uluru from the landscape.

► Uluru is composed of arkose, a type of sandstone rich in quartz and pink minerals called feldspars. The reddish color of the rock is heightened by iron oxides.

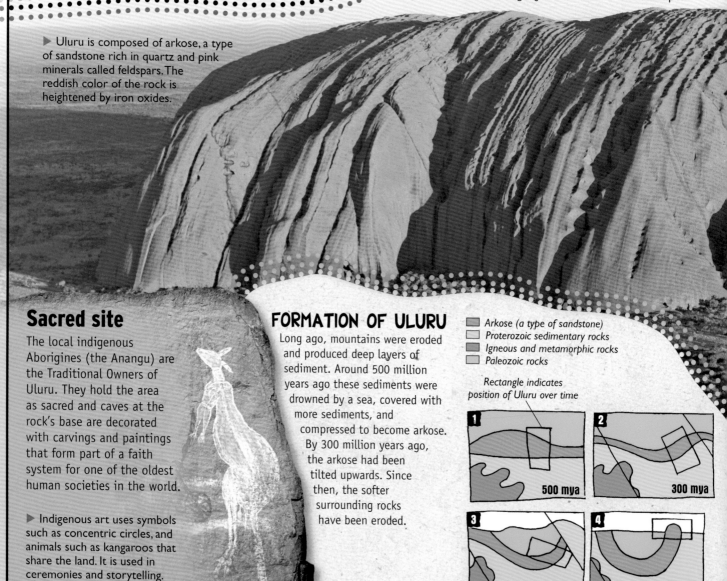

Sacred site

The local indigenous Aborigines (the Anangu) are the Traditional Owners of Uluru. They hold the area as sacred and caves at the rock's base are decorated with carvings and paintings that form part of a faith system for one of the oldest human societies in the world.

► Indigenous art uses symbols such as concentric circles, and animals such as kangaroos that share the land. It is used in ceremonies and storytelling.

FORMATION OF ULURU

Long ago, mountains were eroded and produced deep layers of sediment. Around 500 million years ago these sediments were drowned by a sea, covered with more sediments, and compressed to become arkose. By 300 million years ago, the arkose had been tilted upwards. Since then, the softer surrounding rocks have been eroded.

■ Arkose (a type of sandstone)
□ Proterozoic sedimentary rocks
■ Igneous and metamorphic rocks
■ Paleozoic rocks

Rectangle indicates position of Uluru over time

1 500 mya

2 300 mya

3 65 mya

4 Present

SUN SPECTACULAR

Uluru is known for its astonishing beauty at sunrise and sunset, when the rock takes on a luminous orange glow. As the Sun's rays pass through the atmosphere, they are filtered by dust, ash, and water vapor, especially when the Sun is low in the sky. Blue light rays are blocked, leaving the red end of the light spectrum to illuminate the rock. Uluru's natural red tones intensify the phenomenon.

12 noon

Sunset

Less light is filtered

More light is filtered by atmosphere

The rock contains pink feldspars and red iron oxides

Earth

Many Heads

About 20 mi (32 km) west of Uluru lie 36 steep-sided rock domes. Their Aboriginal name—Kata Tjuta—describes the peaks as "Many Heads." Formed at the same time as Uluru, they are also revered as sacred sites. The largest rock, Mount Olga, gives Kata Tjuta their alternative name—The Olgas.

▼ The resistant rock of Kata Tjuta contains gravel, pebbles, and boulders all held together by a natural cement.

THE DEEP LINES THAT SCORE ULURU'S SURFACE ARE CAUSED BY WIND AND RAIN, WHICH ARE GRADUALLY WEARING AWAY THE ROCK.

Big rock at Burringurrah

Also known as Mount Augustus, Burringurrah is twice the size of Uluru, and much older. This solitary peak is one of the largest rocks in the world with a height of 2,400 ft (around 720 m). It stretches for 5 mi (8 km) and natural springs at its base have long supported the Wadjari Aboriginal people.

▼ The scrubland and waterholes around Burringurrah create a wildlife paradise where gum trees, wildflowers, reptiles, bustards, and even emus thrive.

ROCK
and Awe

▼ Viewed by satellite, the mighty Colorado River looks like a meandering stream within the snow-covered chasm that surrounds it.

The Grand Canyon is a scar on the face of Earth that is visible from space. This long, wide, and very deep chasm is a slice through our planet's mind-boggling history—and it is still growing.

Rainbow rocks

The Grand Canyon forms part of an incredible vista at any time of day, but as the Sun settles behind the distant horizon its fabulous colors become even more evident. Pale pinks and lilacs give way to brilliant reds and neon oranges while the sky becomes an inky wash. Golden light and deep shadows emphasize the canyon's countless ridges, pinnacles, and valleys, highlighting the colossal scale of this breathtaking panorama.

Howdy hoodoo

It's hard to imagine that bizarre amphitheaters of rock populated by needlelike pinnacles (hoodoos) were once vast plateaus of solid rock that have been sculpted by erosion and the weather. Bryce Canyon (below) was named after a pioneer who built a ranch there in the 1870s and remarked that it was a terrible place to lose a cow!

▼ The tallest pinnacle at Bryce Canyon is called Thor's Hammer and is a popular spot for tourists viewing a spectacular sunset.

▲ The view from Toroweap Outlook takes in the Inner Canyon and its heart—the Colorado River.

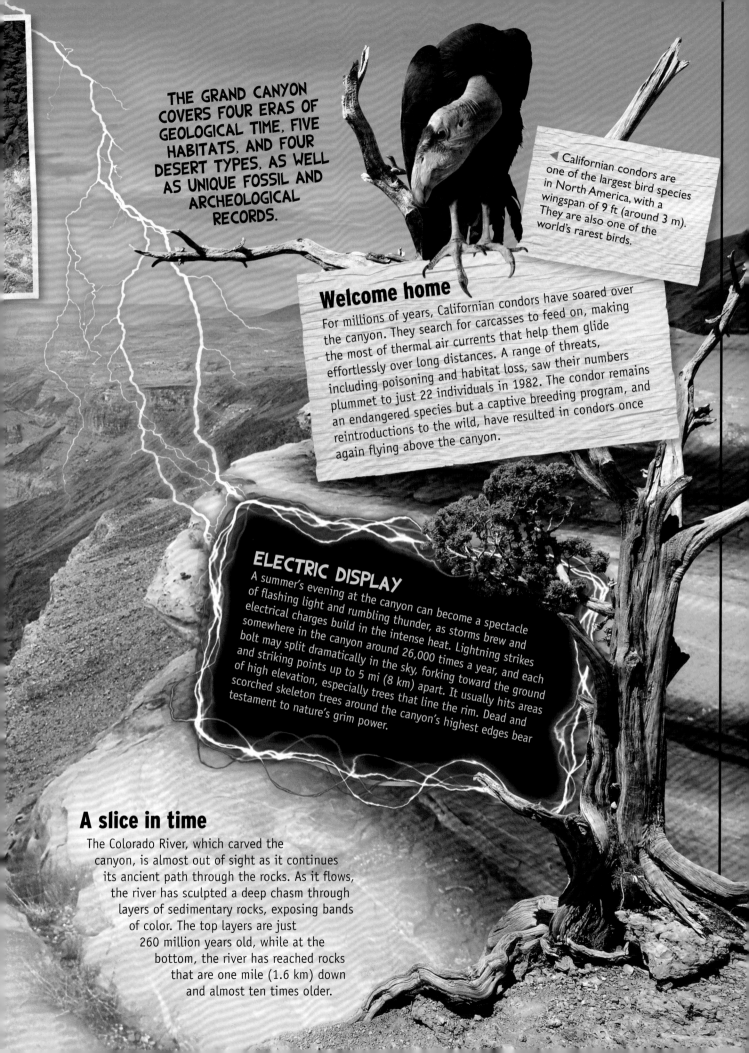

THE GRAND CANYON COVERS FOUR ERAS OF GEOLOGICAL TIME, FIVE HABITATS, AND FOUR DESERT TYPES, AS WELL AS UNIQUE FOSSIL AND ARCHEOLOGICAL RECORDS.

◀ Californian condors are one of the largest bird species in North America, with a wingspan of 9 ft (around 3 m). They are also one of the world's rarest birds.

Welcome home

For millions of years, Californian condors have soared over the canyon. They search for carcasses to feed on, making the most of thermal air currents that help them glide effortlessly over long distances. A range of threats, including poisoning and habitat loss, saw their numbers plummet to just 22 individuals in 1982. The condor remains an endangered species but a captive breeding program, and reintroductions to the wild, have resulted in condors once again flying above the canyon.

ELECTRIC DISPLAY

A summer's evening at the canyon can become a spectacle of flashing light and rumbling thunder, as storms brew and electrical charges build in the intense heat. Lightning strikes somewhere in the canyon around 26,000 times a year, and each bolt may split dramatically in the sky, forking toward the ground and striking points up to 5 mi (8 km) apart. It usually hits areas of high elevation, especially trees that line the rim. Dead and scorched skeleton trees around the canyon's highest edges bear testament to nature's grim power.

A slice in time

The Colorado River, which carved the canyon, is almost out of sight as it continues its ancient path through the rocks. As it flows, the river has sculpted a deep chasm through layers of sedimentary rocks, exposing bands of color. The top layers are just 260 million years old, while at the bottom, the river has reached rocks that are one mile (1.6 km) down and almost ten times older.

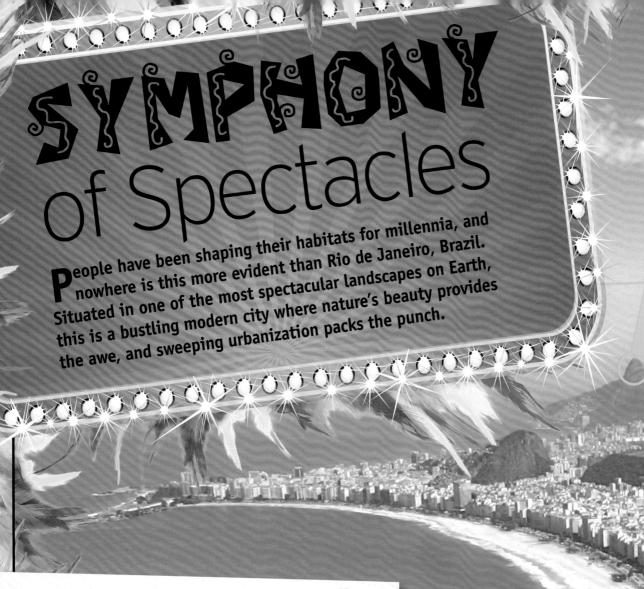

SYMPHONY of Spectacles

People have been shaping their habitats for millennia, and nowhere is this more evident than Rio de Janeiro, Brazil. Situated in one of the most spectacular landscapes on Earth, this is a bustling modern city where nature's beauty provides the awe, and sweeping urbanization packs the punch.

Peachy beaches

Tourists throng Rio's world-famous coast, enjoying the sunshine and sea along the magnificent 2.5 mi (4 km) crescent of white sand that is Copacabana Beach. Here, waterfront hotels, shops, and restaurants are as much part of the scenery as the backdrop of forest-covered hills.

▼ Citizens of Rio, or *Cariocas*, flock to Copacabana Beach in the day to play, swim, and laze in the sunshine, but in the evening, partying takes over.

◄ Sugarloaf Mountain is 1,299 ft (396 m) tall and juts into the sky at the tip of the bay's peninsula.

Landmark peak

Rio is generally agreed to be one of the most stunning harbor cities in the world. Built on a series of hills, Brazil's carnival city is still flanked by swathes of virgin forest and enjoys a stunning view over Guanabara Bay and granite islands. Sugarloaf Mountain, however, has long been the area's iconic feature and is still an ideal landmark for sailors approaching Rio after an arduous journey across the Atlantic.

CABLE CARS HAVE FERRIED ABOUT 37 MILLION VISITORS TO SUGARLOAF SINCE 1912. THEY ENJOY THE JOURNEY OF A LIFETIME AND PANORAMIC VIEWS OF RIO AND ITS BAY.

Rocky Corcovado

Corcovado is a huge granite peak named after the Portuguese word for "hunchback." Both Sugarloaf and Corcovado are volcanic formations that were once underground. Over hundreds of millions of years, the softer rock on top wore away, leaving these strange rocks exposed as steep-sided mountains—so steep that soil cannot form so they remain bare rock. Where the sea has flooded into the gaps between the granite islands as sea levels rose, beautiful curving bays are created.

▲ Tourists visiting Christ the Redeemer have the best views over the city and bay. The statue was built in the Art Deco style and completed in 1931.

CRADLE of Life

One of the most striking natural wonders of the world, the Great Rift Valley extends from Jordan to Mozambique. This enormous system of valleys, lakes, plateaus, mountains, and volcanoes is home to millions of animals and contains Olduvai Gorge, an area of Tanzania regarded as the cradle of human life.

SHIFT AND SHAKE

The Great Rift Valley is the ever-widening gap between two vast tectonic plates that are moving gradually apart. Starting in southwestern Asia, this dramatic steep-sided valley cuts through East Africa, completely dividing every country it passes through. The valley and its landforms extend for 4,000 mi (around 6,500 km) and are also known as the East African Rift System. Already in the north, the sea has flooded in to form the Red Sea—and eventually East Africa will separate from the rest and the Rift Valley will be an ocean.

▼ The grasslands of the Ngorongoro Crater are home for many Maasai people, who practice nomadic pastoralism.

Steep-sided cliffs

Central sunken area has lakes and volcanoes

Direction of plate movement

Continental crust

Mantle

Magma plume

▲ Upwelling heat in Earth's mantle forces plates apart and causes plenty of volcanic activity along the valley floor. As the plates move, brittle rock is put under enormous pressure and breaks along fault lines.

Ngorongoro Crater

In the southern region of the Great Rift Valley lies the Ngorongoro Crater, the remains of an extinct, collapsed volcano. At up to 14 mi (22.5 km) across and 2,000 ft (610 m) deep, it is the world's largest complete and unflooded caldera (collapsed volcanic crater). Its steep sides help to create the crater's own weather system, and within its "walls" a unique ecosystem exists. The wildlife here is largely isolated from bigger populations that live beyond the Ngorongoro.

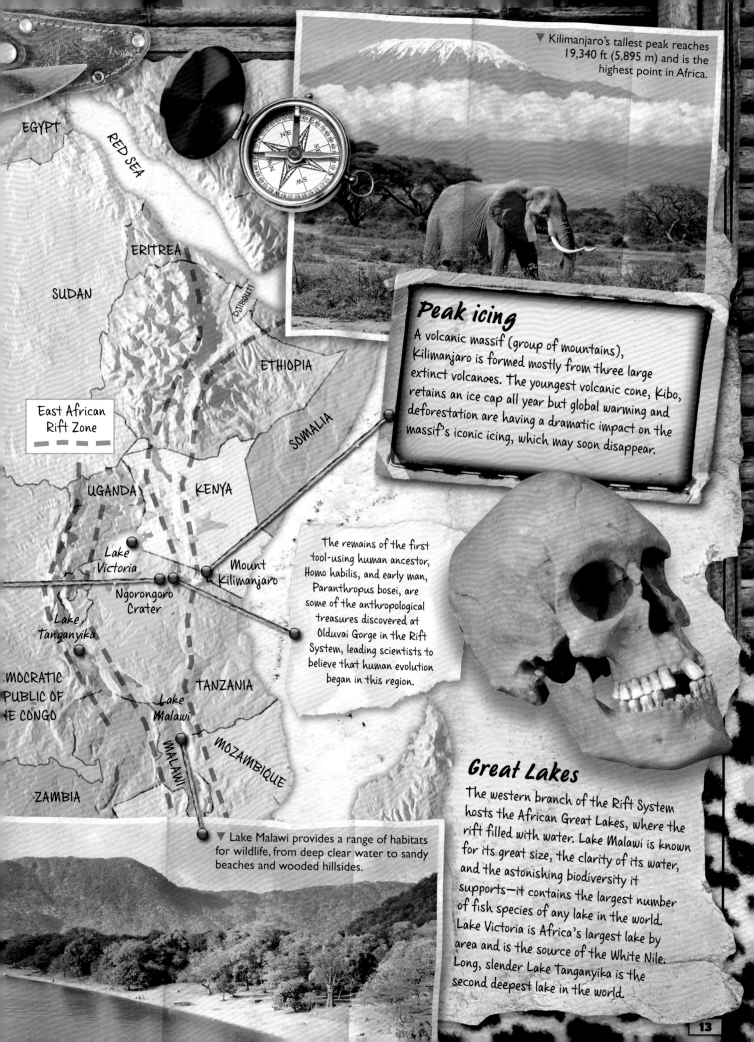

▼ Kilimanjaro's tallest peak reaches 19,340 ft (5,895 m) and is the highest point in Africa.

EGYPT

RED SEA

ERITREA

SUDAN

DJIBOUTI

ETHIOPIA

SOMALIA

East African Rift Zone
- - - -

UGANDA

KENYA

Lake Victoria

Mount Kilimanjaro

Ngorongoro Crater

Lake Tanganyika

DEMOCRATIC REPUBLIC OF THE CONGO

TANZANIA

Lake Malawi

MALAWI

MOZAMBIQUE

ZAMBIA

Peak icing

A volcanic massif (group of mountains), Kilimanjaro is formed mostly from three large extinct volcanoes. The youngest volcanic cone, Kibo, retains an ice cap all year but global warming and deforestation are having a dramatic impact on the massif's iconic icing, which may soon disappear.

The remains of the first tool-using human ancestor, Homo habilis, and early man, Paranthropus bosei, are some of the anthropological treasures discovered at Olduvai Gorge in the Rift System, leading scientists to believe that human evolution began in this region.

▼ Lake Malawi provides a range of habitats for wildlife, from deep clear water to sandy beaches and wooded hillsides.

Great Lakes

The western branch of the Rift System hosts the African Great Lakes, where the rift filled with water. Lake Malawi is known for its great size, the clarity of its water, and the astonishing biodiversity it supports—it contains the largest number of fish species of any lake in the world. Lake Victoria is Africa's largest lake by area and is the source of the White Nile. Long, slender Lake Tanganyika is the second deepest lake in the world.

Wild **Wetland**

The Pantanal is the largest-known freshwater wetland in the world, and it is a paradise for animals and plants. It extends from Brazil into Paraguay and Bolivia, covering at least 50,000 sq mi (129,500 sq km)—an area bigger than 29 of the U.S. states.

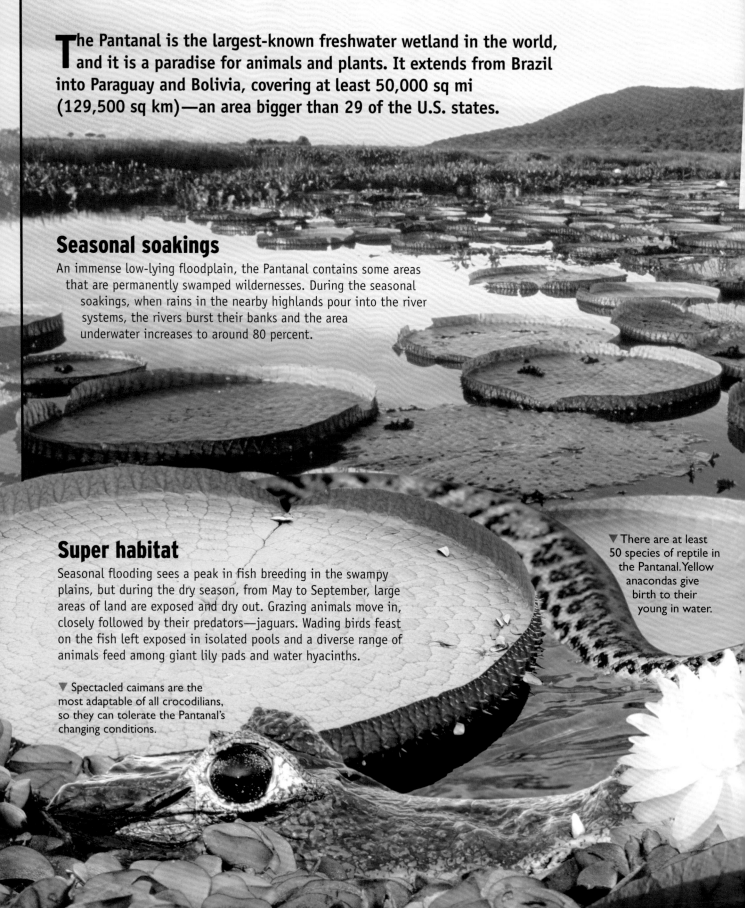

Seasonal soakings

An immense low-lying floodplain, the Pantanal contains some areas that are permanently swamped wildernesses. During the seasonal soakings, when rains in the nearby highlands pour into the river systems, the rivers burst their banks and the area underwater increases to around 80 percent.

Super habitat

Seasonal flooding sees a peak in fish breeding in the swampy plains, but during the dry season, from May to September, large areas of land are exposed and dry out. Grazing animals move in, closely followed by their predators—jaguars. Wading birds feast on the fish left exposed in isolated pools and a diverse range of animals feed among giant lily pads and water hyacinths.

▼ Spectacled caimans are the most adaptable of all crocodilians, so they can tolerate the Pantanal's changing conditions.

▼ There are at least 50 species of reptile in the Pantanal. Yellow anacondas give birth to their young in water.

▼ Floodwaters on the Pantanal can reach 13 ft (4 m) in height during and after the long summer rainy season, creating challenging conditions for cowboys and their herds.

Alien invaders

Cattle have been grazing on the Pantanal for around 260 years and many millions are now kept on enormous ranches. Large areas of woody vegetation have been removed using the cut-and-slash method, or by burning, to produce more grazing land.

▲ An incredible array of wildlife lives on the Pantanal, including the world's largest rodents, capybaras, which have a body length of about 3.3 ft (1 m). They are adept swimmers.

Adios Pantanal?

The Pantanal has been described as "one of the last intact ecological paradises." However, cattle ranching, commercial hunting, and pollution are just a few of the growing threats to this habitat. While some recent large-scale plans to turn the Paraguay River into a more navigable route for cargo have been put on hold, other projects planned for the rivers and tributaries that feed the wetlands are still being developed. This is likely to increase the environmental pressures that already face this precious ecosystem.

"PANTANAL" MEANS "SWAMP," BUT ACTUALLY THE REGION IS A PLAIN, AND THE REMAINS OF AN ANCIENT INLAND SEA THAT IS SLOWLY DRYING OUT.

WHITE Out

▼ Cracks and ridges of edible salt form patterns on the surface of Salar de Uyuni.

The astonishing all-white vista created by a large salt flat makes for a formidable sight. These dried-out lakes are some of Earth's flattest surfaces, and the salt crystals that cover them reflect the Sun's rays to create glimmering, shimmering spectacles.

All dried up

Salar de Uyuni is a huge windswept salt flat high on Bolivia's Altiplano (high plain). It is found at an elevation of 11,995 ft (3,656 m) above sea level and covers an area of 4,085 sq mi (10,580 sq km). Beneath several feet of salt lies a salty pool of water that belonged, around 40,000 years ago, to a much larger body of water—the prehistoric Lake Minchin. Over time, heat has evaporated the water, allowing salt to precipitate out as a solid. Salar de Uyuni receives seasonal flooding, and when covered in a thin film of water it creates one of the world's largest natural mirrors.

Pass the salt

The high concentration of salt in these lakes creates an inhospitable environment, although a few species manage to survive. Salar de Uyuni also supports human life in the form of mining communities and tourism. The mined salt is used in building materials. In the future, mining may concentrate on extracting vast reserves of lithium, which lies beneath the salt-encrusted surface. This soft metal is used primarily by ceramics and glass industries, and in the production of batteries.

◄ Giant cacti grow on Inkahuasi Island, a rocky outcrop in Salar de Uyuni. They have a dense covering of spines, which are modified leaves, and flower periodically.

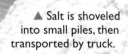

▲ Salt is shoveled into small piles, then transported by truck.

Tiny islands

While the salt plain is almost perfectly flat, there are protrusions that rise above its pristine white surface. These rocky outcrops near the middle of the lake are the remnants of volcanoes that existed on the plain before being flooded by the ancient Lake Minchin. They contain fossils that provide evidence of this region's submerged history, and today they provide an oasis in the sea of vast, blinding whiteness. On these islands hardy animals and plants can survive, including cacti. When the lake is flooded, South American flamingos also visit, to feed and breed.

◀ As the Sun slides toward the horizon, the sheets of white salt take on a stunning blue hue, and rock islands create strange shadows.

SALAR DE UYUNI IS THE WORLD'S LARGEST SALT FLAT, AND THE DIFFERENCE FROM ITS LOWEST PARTS TO ITS HIGHEST PARTS IS NO GREATER THAN 3 FT (80 CM).

TRAIN CEMETERY

Old train tracks connect the lake to the nearby town of Uyuni. Cargoes of salt were taken from the lake to the town by train, and onward to ports. The locomotives are no longer used, but have been left to decay in an area known as the "train cemetery."

DRAGON'S Jewels

At Halong Bay, on the border of Vietnam and China, geology and mythology combine to create a mysterious seascape of limestone pillars, islands, and islets. It was once believed that these strange rocky outcrops were placed there by dragons to defend the land from invasion.

Drowned rocks

During Earth's history the sea level has risen and fallen after the planet's climate has undergone large changes. When seawater is trapped in ice the sea level falls; when global warming occurs the ice melts, and the sea level rises. It was this process that caused the sea to invade a karst (limestone) mountain landscape on the Vietnamese coast, in an area now called the Gulf of Tonkin, and create Halong Bay. The strange shape of the islands comes from the way that limestone is dissolved by acidic rainwater. Today, the bay contains more than 2,000 islands, each covered with virgin jungles. They are still largely uninhabited and unspoilt.

▼ The water in Halong Bay is mostly less than 30 ft (around 10 m) deep, and covers a drowned karst plain.

▼ As acid rain erodes the islands they can develop into unusual shapes, giving rise to their local names, such as "Elephant" and "Wallowing Buffalo."

Jade and jewels

According to ancient legend, Halong Bay was formed when the region was under invasion, and dragons came to defend the land. As they descended from the sky, the dragons spat out thousands of pearls. Each pearl hit the water and turned into a jade island, and together the islands created an impenetrable barrier to the invading ships.

Caves of awe

Marine erosion has continued to shape and form the landscape, carving out many more caves and grottoes, adding to those created before the coast was flooded. Hang Sung Sot ("Cave of Awe"), for example, is one of the oldest caves in the area and has passages that are more than 33 ft (10 m) high and wide that lead downward to caves filled with stalagmites and boulders.

THE TOWERS OF LIMESTONE HAVE NEAR-VERTICAL SIDES. ROCKFALLS ARE COMMON AND HUGE SLABS OF ROCK OFTEN PEEL OFF AND SLAM INTO THE SEA BELOW.

THE INVADING SEA

Rain falling on limestone creates acid, which dissolves the rock and creates tunnels, caves, and shafts called sinkholes. When the sea invades, this "drowned karst" landscape is the result.

Older caves formed when the sea level was higher

Hills

Chasm

Tower

Recently formed cave

Drowned chasm

PINNACLEs and Pillars

When the world's weathering processes get to work, the landscape can be utterly transformed. Changes in air temperature, and moisture and chemicals in the atmosphere, can carve strange pillars, columns, and pinnacles from solid stone, producing a spectacular range of scenery.

▼ Parts of Cappadocia's bizarre landscape are protected within the boundaries of the Goreme National Park in Turkey.

Fairy chimneys

In Turkey's Cappadocia region, thousands of conical structures appear to rise out of the ground, reaching up to 165 ft (50 m) in height. These are the remains of a vast blanket of volcanic ash that solidified into a soft rock called tuff. Over millions of years, erosion has removed much of the tuff and sculpted these towers, which are known as fairy chimneys. More resistant rock forms mushroomlike caps on some of them.

Twelve Apostles

Coastal rock stacks are witnesses to the immense ability of the sea to carve solid rock. The Twelve Apostles in Australia are limestone stacks that stand along a high-energy coast. They were once part of a large limestone bed that has been slowly demolished by wind, waves, and rain. They continue to disappear at a rate of one inch (2.5 cm) a year.

▲ Australia's Twelve Apostles were originally known as The Sow and her Pigs, before being renamed in the 1950s.

The Needles

When Lot's Wife, a 120 ft (37 m) sea stack in coastal waters by the Isle of Wight, collapsed into the sea during a storm in the 18th century, it was said that the sound could be heard miles away. Lot's Wife was tall and thin, which is why the group of sea stacks it belonged to are known as The Needles, even though the three remaining stacks are quite stumpy. A lighthouse clings to the furthermost Needle, to warn shipping of the collapsed stack below the waves.

▼ The Needles in southern England are formed of chalk, a soft, white limestone.

Moonscape on Earth

The Pinnacles Desert in Australia has a spectral quality, and it is often compared to a scene from a science fiction movie. At sunset the stone structures rise from a bed of golden sand and are set against a sky that is washed in pinks, golds, and lilacs. The Pinnacles were formed recently in geological time and they are the remains of a limestone bed that has been eroded, chemically changed by rainwater, and further altered by plants.

▲ The tallest structures in the Pinnacles Desert are 11.5 ft (3.5 m) tall.

Bald Heads

The large balancing boulders at Matobo Hills in Zimbabwe have been called Ama Tobo, or Bald Heads. They are made of granite, which formed under intense heat and pressure during a volcanic mountain-building phase. Cracks in the rock have helped the elements erode the boulders into these strange shapes. Cecil Rhodes, the founder of Rhodesia—now Zimbabwe and Zambia—is buried here.

▼ Stacks of rocks defy gravity at Matobo Hills.

Smoke that THUNDERS

As the mighty Zambezi River plunges over a vertical cliff-edge, a thunderous roar fills the chasm below. A vast, white veil of mist plumes upward, giving the Victoria Falls its local name of *Mosi-oa-Tunya*, which means "The Smoke that Thunders."

Falling sheets

The Victoria Falls is neither the tallest nor the widest waterfall, but it can lay claim to producing the largest single sheet of water in the world. In full flood, during February and March, more than 18 million cu ft (500,000 cu m) of water cascades over the precipice every second. Sited at the border of Zambia and Zimbabwe, the falls span nearly 6,000 ft (1,800 m) at the widest point, and have a maximum drop of 355 ft (108 m).

▼ The Victoria Falls cascades over the lip of a large rocky plateau. The mass of water has been slicing slowly through this rock for two million years.

Gouging gorges

After the water pummels the rocks at the bottom of the Victoria Falls, it continues its journey through a narrow zigzag series of gorges, passing seven points where the falls were once sited. Water erosion continues to gouge out weaker areas in a vast plateau of basalt rock, moving the falls further and further up the river's course.

▶ After descending the falls, the wide Zambezi is forced through a long zigzag series of extremely narrow chasms, increasing the speed and force of the water's flow.

Devil's Pool

Tourists flock to the Victoria Falls and, when the river levels drop, those looking for an adrenaline rush can enjoy the surreal—and risky—experience of bathing on a cliff edge. The Devil's Pool has a natural rock wall that (in theory) prevents swimmers from being dragged over the top by the raging water's momentum.

▲ Low water levels between September and December allow tourists to enter the Devil's Pool and swim perilously close to the falls' edge.

THE VICTORIA FALLS IS ABOUT TWICE AS WIDE AND DEEP AS THE NIAGARA FALLS. ITS SHIMMERING MIST CAN BE SEEN MORE THAN 12 MI (20 KM) AWAY.

Angel Falls

The best way to appreciate the awesome spectacle of the world's tallest falls is by air. In fact, the Angel Falls in Venezuela was named after U.S. pilot Jimmy Angel, who got a bird's-eye view when he crash-landed nearby in 1937. The Churún River gushes over the Angel Falls at such a rate that water scarcely touches the cliff face as it plummets 3,212 ft (979 m).

▲ In Venezuela the Angel Falls is known as *Kerepakupai Merú*, which means "waterfall of the deepest place."

CARNIVAL
of Coral

The enormous size of the Great Barrier Reef needs a long-distance view because its thousands of individual reefs and islands stretch for over 1,240 mi (2,000 km). Getting to grips with its astounding impact on nature, however, means going underwater.

▼ The reef is made up of 3,000 smaller reefs and 1,000 islands.

Slow-grow

A reef is a slow-growing structure of rocky carbonate compounds and the living coral polyps that create them. Australia's Great Barrier Reef is the planet's most extensive coral-reef system and one of the largest structures ever made by living things. The reef has been growing for 18 million years. The living parts, which are growing on top of the older sections, began forming after the last Ice Age, 8,000–20,000 years ago.

1. Planula searches for a place to settle

2. Planula attaches to a hard surface

▼ Polyps can reproduce in two ways. An egg can grow into a planula, or an adult can make a bud, which grows into a twin of itself.

3. Polyp begins to grow a stony cup

4. Coral colony begins to grow through "budding"

▲ Yonge Reef is a popular part of the Great Barrier Reef for divers because of the huge diversity of its corals and other wildlife.

Critical critters

Coral polyps are soft-bodied animals related to sea anemones. They live in extensive colonies and secrete minerals to create protective cups around themselves. It is these cups that make up the bulk of a reef structure. Corals that grow near the surface in sunlit waters have a symbiotic relationship with zooxanthellae algae. The corals provide the algae with carbon dioxide, nutrients, and a safe place to live; the algae give the corals sugar and oxygen from photosynthesis.

THE SINGLE BIGGEST THREAT TO CORAL REEFS IS THOUGHT TO BE POLLUTION, BUT THIS FRAGILE ECOSYSTEM IS EASILY DAMAGED AND IS AT RISK FROM NUMEROUS FACTORS, INCLUDING TOURISM AND GLOBAL WARMING.

REEF ENCOUNTERS

Islanders from the Torres Strait and Aborigines from Australia have been fishing around the Barrier Reef for more than 60,000 years. They are now known as the Traditional Owners of the Great Barrier Reef, and work to conserve the region's biodiversity, and its cultural history. Scientists began studying the reef in the 18th century, after the ship of British explorer James Cook ran aground on the coral.

▲ Nautiluses have scarcely changed in millions of years, and are considered to be living fossils.

Rain forest of the sea

A journey under the sea reveals another magical side to the reef: in the silence of the turquoise waters an underwater carnival of colors is revealed. The reef provides a habitat for an enormous range of wildlife, producing an astonishing level of biodiversity. Schools of tiny silvery fish dart between the weirdly shaped corals, and on their rocky surfaces there are pink mollusks, blue starfish, purple anemones, transparent shrimps, and garish worms. Large predators, such as sharks and squid, venture close to shore to feed and breed. The coral provides plenty of hiding places.

◀ Sweetlips fish undergo incredible color transformations as they age, often becoming less colorful but more boldly patterned.

▼ Jellyfish are closely related to the coral polyps that build the reef. They move with a pulsing rhythm and catch animals in their stinging tentacles.

Valley of **THE MOON**

Captivatingly beautiful in its austerity, Wadi Rum has inspired many writers to attempt to describe the maze of skyscraper-like monoliths that rise from the desert sand. Part of this landscape's spectacular impact comes from the play of light on the rocks, and the life-giving effect of water in an arid land.

Vast valleys

The Wadi Rum valley cuts through south Jordan. Layers of beige, orange, red, and gray sedimentary sandstones rest upon an ancient layer of granite that is more than 2,000 million years old. The tectonic events that continue to shape the Great Rift Valley have tilted and fractured the sandstones, which have been eroded by wind and rain into stone sculptures, arches, and canyons.

▼ One of the rock formations in Wadi Rum was named after T. E. Lawrence's book *The Seven Pillars of Wisdom*—although the seven pillars in the book have no connection with Wadi Rum.

◀ ▼ Desert scenes in the 1962 movie, *Lawrence of Arabia*, were shot in Wadi Rum, which was the original location of much of the historical action.

Lawrence of Arabia

Wadi Rum was an important site during World War I (1914–1918) when the Arabs were in revolt against the Ottomans. Prince Faisal Bin Hussein and British soldier T. E. Lawrence (known as Lawrence of Arabia) made their base here.

COLUMBIA PICTURES presents THE SAM SPIEGEL · DAVID LEAN Production of

LAWRENCE OF ARABIA

WINNER OF 7 ACADEMY AWARDS

STARRING

ALEC GUINNESS · ANTHONY QUINN · JACK HAWKINS
ANTHONY QUAYLE · CLAUDE RAINS · ARTHUR KENNEDY
WITH
OMAR SHARIF as 'ALI' and introducing **PETER O'TOOLE** 'LAWRENCE'

Spring awakening

After the winter rains, Wadi Rum's natural springs swell, causing the desert to explode with life. Plants such as poppies and black irises bloom in the usually barren ground, and hardy animals such as snakes, ibex, gray wolves, and foxes also survive in the harsh landscape.

▼ The desert lark is one of more than 100 bird species that have been recorded at Wadi Rum.

▶ Crocuses rest as corms during dry periods, but grow and flower after rainfall.

A POPULAR MOVIE LOCATION, WADI RUM WAS USED TO PORTRAY THE SURFACE OF MARS IN "RED PLANET" (2000) AND EGYPT IN "TRANSFORMERS: REVENGE OF THE FALLEN" (2009).

▼ The tectonic events that continue to shape the Rift Valley have tilted and fractured the sandstones of Wadi Rum. They have been eroded by wind, rain, and flash floods into red cliffs and deep canyons.

▼ Jordan's Desert Patrol still sends its famous Camel Corps to police areas of the Wadi Rum where even Land Rovers cannot reach.

Intrepid travelers

People have been traveling through this desert for millennia. Many of them have left archeological evidence that hints at the region's rich history, from flint axes and prehistoric rock carvings to the remains of a 2,000-year-old temple built by Nabataean people. Today, tribal Bedouins still herd their goats through the canyons, camping in goat-hair tents when following their traditional nomadic lifestyle.

ICE Mountains

In Europe, the Alps form a vast mountain barrier. They dominate the continent, shaping its land and even affecting its culture and history. Although they are situated in a temperate region, the Alps endure lashing ice storms in winter and the peaks stay snowy all year round.

Pyramid peak

With its steep, angular peak the Matterhorn is Europe's iconic mountain—easy to recognize and with a dangerous reputation. Despite its height, the Matterhorn's four faces are virtually snowless because of their steepness. The first ascent of the mountain took place in 1865, with a loss of four lives. Since then, many hundreds more climbers have died scaling its heights, and the Matterhorn still has one of the highest death rates in the world.

▲ The Matterhorn straddles the border between Switzerland and Italy and is 14,693 ft (4,478 m) tall. Italians call it *Monte Cervino*. It requires great technical skill to climb because the rock is unstable, and variable weather conditions prevail.

▼ As the glacier grinds onward, the combination of the great weight of ice and the rocks inside it scours the landscape.

Making mountains

The Alps are 650 mi (about 1,050 km) long and up to 120 mi (about 200 km) wide. Several Alpine mountains are more than 13,000 ft (4,000 m) tall, and the tallest is Mont Blanc in France. The range began to form about 90 million years ago when two tectonic plates began to converge. The plates crushed and folded the layers of rock between them, forcing them into mountains and valleys, which have been eroded and shaped by glaciation in the last two million years.

Great glaciers

The Aletsch Glacier is an enormous frozen river of ice moving slowly southward from Alpine peaks toward the Rhône Valley. Although it is moving downhill because of gravity, the glacier's front is retreating because it melts as it comes down into warmer air. Water flowing under the ice causes the glacier to deposit its cargo of rocks, creating sediments known as moraines. The Aletsch is Europe's largest valley glacier, measuring 16 mi (25 km), although it has retreated about 2 mi (3 km) in the last 150 years.

▼ The flowers in an Alpine meadow are usually small and low-growing to minimize damage from winds and frosts. They help to create stunning summer panoramas, with backdrops of snow-tipped mountains.

Alpine meadows

Even mighty mountains are not strong enough to withstand the weather. Over millions of years rain, ice, wind, and snow eroded the Alpine rocks, gradually turning them, with organic debris, into soil that can support meadows. The high Alpine meadows are relatively inaccessible, and are now some of Europe's least spoilt habitats. Seemingly fragile plants can survive under snow during winter, then burst into life when the snow melts, creating a dazzling carpet of flowers.

WILDLIFE
Hideaway

The island of Madagascar is a place like no other—literally. It broke away from Africa 150–180 million years ago and now exists as a mini-continent of natural wonders with a bewilderingly diverse range of landscapes and wildlife.

MASSIVE MASSIF

An enormous sheer rock face draws adventurers to central Madagascar. Known as the Tsaranoro Massif, the 2,600-ft (800-m) granite cliff is almost vertical, making it an interesting challenge for climbers, and an awesome spot for the bravest paragliders and base jumpers.

▲ With nowhere to camp out, climbers aim to climb the granite cliffs of Tsaranoro in just one day. The rock faces are solid without cracks, so climbers drill bolts into the cliff to ascend new routes.

M A D

SPLITTING UP

At 226,662 sq mi (587,051 sq km) in area, Madagascar is Earth's fourth largest island but it was once part of a giant landmass called Gondwana. Around 180 million years ago a chunk of eastern Gondwana began to move away from Africa. More separations followed, forming Antarctica, India, Australia, and Madagascar.

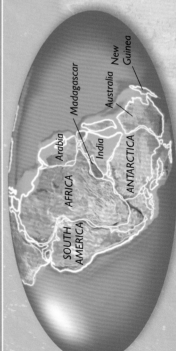

▲ Gondwana was one of two supercontinents that would eventually split into smaller landmasses. It contained most of the landmasses that are in today's Southern Hemisphere, including Madagascar (red).

TREASURE TROVES

Separated from the rest of the world, Madagascar embarked on its own evolutionary journey, and most of the species of animals and plants found here live nowhere else. Although much of Madagascar's rain forest has been felled, the remaining areas still harbor 8,000 species of endemic plants, more than 1,000 types of spider, and about 300 species of frog.

▼ Watery habitats are home to many amphibians and fish.

G A S C A R

LEMURS ALL ALONE

The first mammals arrived about 60 million years ago, long after the island had been formed. It is thought they arrived on rafts of floating vegetation, and their evolutionary progress continued down a different path to those they had left behind. About 40 species of lemurs, a type of primate with large eyes and foxlike faces, evolved here.

▲ Brown lemurs rarely leave the forest canopy, and feed on fruit, leaves, tree sap, and bugs.

TSINGY LANDS

Parts of Madagascar are virtually impenetrable, where razor-sharp pyramids of rock emerge from the ground. The rocks are so closely packed together it is difficult to find a path between them. They are known as "tsingy" locally, because they make a bell-like sound when struck.

▼ The tsingy peaks were molded by the chemical reaction between rainwater and limestone.

▼ The Avenue of the Baobabs was once surrounded by lush forest.

UPSIDE-DOWN TREES

Peculiar baobabs are the iconic trees of the island. Their swollen trunks hold huge stores of water to help the plants get through the dry season, and some baobabs have lived for more than 1,000 years. Lemurs and giant moths suck nectar from their flowers. There are eight species of baobab, and six of them live only on Madagascar.

31

frozen Kingdom

Carved by glaciers and exposed to some of Earth's most menacing weather, Svalbard is home to one of the planet's last great wildernesses. This collection of islands lies inside the Arctic Circle and encounters extraordinary phenomena, including the Northern Lights.

▲ Aurorae occur at heights of 50–600 mi (80–1000 km) above Earth, and these silent, flickering displays can be any combination of green, yellow, blue, and red.

Glacier on the move

About 80 percent of Spitsbergen, the main island in Svalbard, is covered by glaciers. One of the most famous of these is Kongsvegen. This mighty river of ice covers about 40 sq mi (105 sq km) and has a length of about 12 mi (20 km). As its low-lying tip, or terminus, reaches the sea, enormous chunks of ice break off to form icebergs.

▲ As Kongsvegen reaches the sea it extends into the Kongsfjorden (a fjord) and icebergs (in the foreground) break away.

▲ The molecular structure of ice is less dense than that of liquid water. This means that icebergs can float in seas and rivers.

Archipelago of ice

Spitsbergen's snowcapped Tre-Kroner Mountains give way to a huge inlet called Kongsfjorden, where ice-cold Arctic waters meet the warmer Atlantic Ocean. Enormous icebergs litter the entrance of the fjord, but the warmer waters entice an unexpected array of wildlife to the area, from fulmars to black-legged kittiwakes. In summer, up to three million birds flock to Svalbard, where they are able to feed for 24 hours when the midnight Sun lights up the land, even during the dead of night.

Northern Lights

Under a still, cold winter's sky, one of the most extraordinary reminders of the planet's place in a bigger Universe is often on view. The Northern Lights, or *Aurora Borealis*, are fleeting visible displays of electrical and magnetic forces. Sheets of light move across the star-studded sky, and their sweeping spectral colors indicate that electric particles from solar winds are splitting oxygen and nitrogen-based molecules in the atmosphere.

IN 1925 EXPLORER ROALD AMUNDSEN ATTEMPTED TO FLY FROM SVALBARD TO THE NORTH POLE IN A DORNIER WAL FLYING BOAT—AND FAILED.

Sparkling snowbows

When sunlight hits rain it can trigger a rainbow, and when it hits flakes of falling snow, a rare sight—the snowbow—may result. Ice crystals in snow bend, or refract, light rays causing them to separate into their constituent rainbow colors.

▶ Snowbows are rare phenomena because they only form in conditions of bright sunlight and light snow.

▼ Polar bears take what they can find. This predator is scavenging on the remains of a fin whale.

Arctic hunters

Svalbard is shared by humans and other mammals that are better equipped to withstand the extreme weather. Polar bears are one of the few mammals that will actively hunt humans, although they usually feed on seals instead. They roam over huge areas in Svalbard, and are as adept at swimming as they are at walking over vast expanses of ice.

Big Island's FIRE

Many of Earth's most awesome features and processes lie hidden beneath its surface. At volcanic hotspots, however, the majestic power of our planet is on view, and there are few better places to witness it than in Hawaii.

HAWAII'S BIG ISLAND

According to Native Hawaiian mythology, when Pele—the goddess of volcanoes—is angry she stamps her feet, causing earthquakes, and starts volcanic eruptions with a shake of her magic stick. If the myth is true, Pele must be furious with Hawaii's Big Island—this is a record-breaking volcanic hotspot without equal on Earth.

MAUNA LOA

- The world's largest active volcano.
- Dome is 64 miles (103 km) across.
- One of the biggest single mountains in the world.
- In 1950, a lava flow from a single fissure devastated a nearby village.

Aloha Mauna Loa

Mauna Loa's great mass covers more than half of Hawaii's Big Island. Its first well-documented eruption occurred in 1843 and Mauna Loa has erupted more than 30 times since. By radiocarbon-dating the lava, scientists have discovered that the first eruption occurred up to one million years ago—and it is almost certain that it will erupt again.

▼ Lava fountains on Mauna Loa spew out from fissures during an eruption. The lava is almost fluid, so it flows easily.

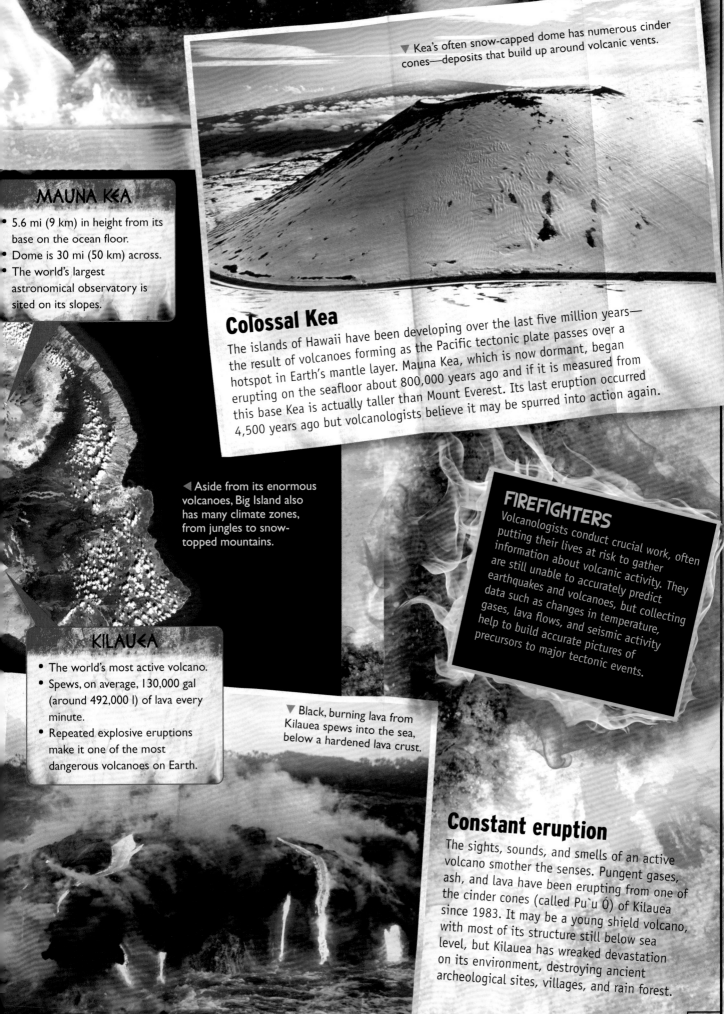

▼ Kea's often snow-capped dome has numerous cinder cones—deposits that build up around volcanic vents.

MAUNA KEA

- 5.6 mi (9 km) in height from its base on the ocean floor.
- Dome is 30 mi (50 km) across.
- The world's largest astronomical observatory is sited on its slopes.

Colossal Kea

The islands of Hawaii have been developing over the last five million years— the result of volcanoes forming as the Pacific tectonic plate passes over a hotspot in Earth's mantle layer. Mauna Kea, which is now dormant, began erupting on the seafloor about 800,000 years ago and if it is measured from this base Kea is actually taller than Mount Everest. Its last eruption occurred 4,500 years ago but volcanologists believe it may be spurred into action again.

◄ Aside from its enormous volcanoes, Big Island also has many climate zones, from jungles to snow-topped mountains.

FIREFIGHTERS

Volcanologists conduct crucial work, often putting their lives at risk to gather information about volcanic activity. They are still unable to accurately predict earthquakes and volcanoes, but collecting data such as changes in temperature, gases, lava flows, and seismic activity help to build accurate pictures of precursors to major tectonic events.

KILAUEA

- The world's most active volcano.
- Spews, on average, 130,000 gal (around 492,000 l) of lava every minute.
- Repeated explosive eruptions make it one of the most dangerous volcanoes on Earth.

▼ Black, burning lava from Kilauea spews into the sea, below a hardened lava crust.

Constant eruption

The sights, sounds, and smells of an active volcano smother the senses. Pungent gases, ash, and lava have been erupting from one of the cinder cones (called Pu`u Ó) of Kilauea since 1983. It may be a young shield volcano, with most of its structure still below sea level, but Kilauea has wreaked devastation on its environment, destroying ancient archeological sites, villages, and rain forest.

EMERALD Scene

In 3,000 places on Mexico's Yucatán Peninsula the Sun's warming rays pass through pools or shafts known as cenotes. These holes in the landscape are entrance points to a spectacular underworld that features flooded caverns, ancient Mayan ceremonial altars, and blind fish.

▶ Lush tropical vegetation surrounds Yucatán's cenotes, thanks to a plentiful supply of groundwater in the region.

Sun-filled basins

In Yucatán, most of these caverns contain pools of sparkling groundwater that is incredibly clean, having been filtered by its passage through the limestone. In some places, shafts of light reach down into the caverns, and plants are able to grow. Deep pools of water are home to species of blind fish, and colonies of bats roost along dark stone ledges.

◀ Belize slider turtles feed on vegetation in cenotes, but can clamber out to bask in the sunlight.

The Place of Fear

Few rivers run across the land above this subterranean structure, as all the water flows down holes and into the caverns beneath, in some instances creating cenotes. These wells had great meaning to the Mayans who lived here—they were seen as gateways to the underworld, known as *Xibalba*, or the "Place of Fear." Some cenotes were used as water sources, but others were used for the purpose of sacrifice, and people were thrown into the pools to appease the god of rain.

▲ This ancient skull was found in a cenote, and was possibly that of a human sacrifice victim.

Big impact

The surrounding rock was once part of a giant limestone plain, which was probably damaged by the Chicxulub meteorite that fell here around 65 million years ago, sparking the demise of the dinosaurs. The rock plateau has been further weakened and dissolved by rainwater. Over time, small caves and tunnels have collapsed, creating enormous caverns.

VISION IS OF NO USE TO LITTLE DAMA FISH LIVING IN DARK CENOTES, SO OVER TIME THEY HAVE LOST THEIR EYES.

Flower caves

About 300 mi (500 km) of the caves and watery tunnels have been mapped so far. The largest caves at Yucatán are called Loltun Caves, and their name derives from the Mayan words for "stone flower." Stalactites in these caves create a bell-like chime when struck, and archeological finds suggest that the caves were first inhabited 7,000 years ago.

◀ The limestone structures in the Gran Cenote are often compared to a tiny city of skyscrapers.

WONDER
No More

We are changing our planet at a rate that has only been equalled in the past by cataclysmic events, such as massive meteorite impacts and supervolcano eruptions. Only future generations will fully comprehend the damage we are doing to some of Earth's most awesome places.

▼ Parts of Virunga National Park have been devastated by the clearing of land for farming using "slash-and-burn."

War-torn wilderness

Despite suffering a century of poaching and years of war, the small population of mountain gorillas in Virunga National Park, in the Democratic Republic of the Congo, clings to life. However, the habitat is under relentless pressure from the growing human population, and large areas of forest have been destroyed.

▶ The Virunga National Park is the oldest reserve in Africa and is home to around 100 mountain gorillas.

▼ Varieties of coral create a carpet of colors. Their unusual shapes give rise to common names, such as brain, lettuce, fan, and star coral.

Watery grave

The corals of Belize have been described as the most outstanding barrier reef in the Northern Hemisphere and a significant habitat for endangered species, such as marine turtles, manatees, and American marine crocodiles.

▲ Belize corals are being bleached (killed) by a combination of pollution and rising temperatures.

Dead and gone

The Dead Sea has been shrinking for 10,000 years, but in just 25 years its area has diminished by one fifth. As more water is extracted from the River Jordan, less reaches the Dead Sea. Water is also removed for salt production.

▼ The Dead Sea is a landlocked hypersaline lake between Israel and Jordan.

▼ A pumping station removes water from the Dead Sea to evaporation pools, so salts can be extracted.

◀ Slash pines growing in the freshwater areas of Florida create a habitat for birds and small mammals. The timber is also of commercial use.

Everglades forever?

For the last 70 years, developers have been draining Florida's Everglades swamps to build on the reclaimed land, and water has been diverted from the swamps to supply agriculture and urban areas. The effects have been described as environmental ruin.

▲ Housing developments on the Everglades replace precious habitats and destroy entire ecosystems.

INDEX